Water Cycle

Monica Hughes

www.heinemann.co.uk/library

Visit our website to find out more information about **Heinemann Library** books.

To order:
☎ Phone 44 (0) 1865 888066
🖹 Send a fax to 44 (0) 1865 314091
💻 Visit the Heinemann Bookshop at www.heinemann.co.uk/library to browse our catalogue and order online.

First published in Great Britain by Heinemann Library, Halley Court, Jordan Hill, Oxford OX2 8EJ, part of Harcourt Education. Heinemann is a registered trademark of Harcourt Education Ltd.

© Harcourt Education Ltd 2004.
First published in paperback in 2005.
The moral right of the proprietor has been asserted.

All rights reserved. No part of this publication may be reproduced, stored in a retrieval system, or transmitted in any form or by any means, electronic, mechanical, photocopying, recording, or otherwise, without either the prior written permission of the Publishers or a licence permitting restricted copying in the United Kingdom issued by the Copyright Licensing Agency Ltd, 90 Tottenham Court Road, London W1T 4LP (www.cla.co.uk).

Editorial: Jilly Attwood, Kate Bellamy
Design: Jo Hinton-Malivoire
Picture research: Ginny Stroud-Lewis, Ruth Blair
Production: Séverine Ribierre

Originated by Ambassador Litho Ltd
Printed and bound in China by South China Printing Company

ISBN 978 0 431 11393 7 (hardback)
08 07 06 05 04
10 9 8 7 6 5 4 3 2 1

ISBN 978 0 431 11399 9 (paperback)
09 08
10 9 8 7 6 5 4 3

British Library Cataloguing in Publication Data
Hughes, Monica
Water Cycle - (Nature's Patterns)
551.4'8
A full catalogue record for this book is available from the British Library.

Acknowledgements
The Publishers would like to thank the following for permission to reproduce photographs: Alamy p. **10-11**; Alamy p. **4** (Roberto Contini); Corbis p. **25**; Corbis pp. **16** (Craig Aurness), **13** (Rebecca Emery), **12** (Julie Habel), **6** (Roy Morsch), **24** (David Muench), **15**, **19**, **26**, **27** (Royalty Free), **18** (Alan Schein), **5** (Michael S Yamashita); Getty Images pp. **9**, **21**; John Cleare p. **28**; Getty Images/Photodisc p. **7**, **14**, **20**; Tudor Photography p. **8**, **29**, **30**; Wilderness Photo Library p. **17** (John Noble).

Cover photograph of Mount Rainier, USA, is reproduced with permission of Corbis.

Our thanks to David Lewin for his assistance in the preparation of this book.

Every effort has been made to contact copyright holders of any material reproduced in this book. Any omissions will be rectified in subsequent printings if notice is given to the Publishers.

The paper used to print this book comes from sustainable resources.

Contents

Words appearing in the text in bold, **like this**, are explained in the Glossary.

 Find out more about Nature's Patterns at www.heinemannexplore.co.uk

Nature's patterns

Nature is always changing. Many of the changes follow a **pattern**. This means that they happen over and over again.

Every time we turn on a tap we have fresh clean water.

Water falls from the sky as rain.

Some patterns are called cycles. Cycle patterns go round and round. They have no clear beginning or end. The water cycle is a pattern like this.

5

Water is special

Water is a **liquid**. It is all around us in oceans, rivers and rain. We can see it and feel it. It moves and flows.

Water is a liquid we can taste and feel.

Water always flows downwards.

Water can also change and take different forms. We see these changes and different forms in the water cycle.

7

Water in the air

There is water all around us even when we cannot see it. It is in the air as an **invisible gas** called **water vapour**.

Steam from a boiling pan disappears into the air.

There is less water vapour in cold air and more in warm air. If there is a lot of water vapour in the air it is **humid**.

People use fans to help cool them down when it is humid.

Oceans and seas

The world's oceans and seas are an important part of the water cycle. Heat from the Sun warms the **surface** of the seas and oceans.

When the water becomes warm it begins to **evaporate**. It changes from a **liquid** into the **gas** called **water vapour**.

Water is evaporating from the surface of the sea all the time.

Evaporation on land

Water **evaporates** from streams, rivers, lakes and ponds. It also evaporates from wet roads and puddles, and from the **surfaces** of plants and trees.

The washing dries as the water in the clothes evaporates.

As water evaporates it changes into **water vapour**. All over the land water is evaporating and changing into water vapour.

Water evaporates from rivers and streams.

Clouds

When warm air meets cooler air, the **water vapour** in the air changes from a **gas** to a **liquid**. This is called **condensation**.

Clouds containing drops of water form over the sea.

Clouds change shape depending on how much water is in them.

Water vapour cools and changes into tiny drops of water. This makes clouds. As the air gets cooler the tiny drops join together and fall as rain.

Mountain clouds

Some clouds are blown towards mountains. The mountains force the clouds higher, where the air is cooler. The clouds get heavy with rain.

Mountain areas often have more rain.

Usually rain falls on the side of the mountain that faces the sea. The other side has much less rain. This side is called the rain shadow.

This side of the mountain is the rain shadow. It has less rain and cloud.

17

Rain

Most rain falls back into the sea and the ocean. It then begins to **evaporate**. In this way the water cycle goes round and round.

Rain falling in towns and cities flows back to the sea.

Heavy rain brings extra water to rivers and waterfalls.

Rain soaks into the soil and drains into rivers. Rain falls on rivers and flows back to the sea. The water goes round in a **pattern**.

Snow

When it is very cold the water droplets in clouds **freeze** and change to form **solid ice crystals**. These join together as snowflakes and fall from the clouds as snow.

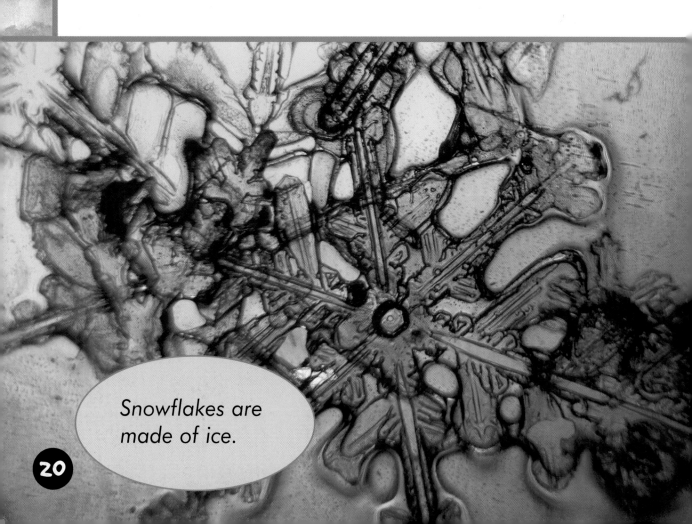

Snowflakes are made of ice.

Snow and ice are water in solid form.

When snow **melts** it changes back to water. Water from the melted snow ends up flowing back to the sea.

The complete cycle

The water cycle goes round and round just like a wheel. Water **evaporates** and changes to **water vapour**.

Water vapour rises and cools to form clouds

The Sun's heat evaporates water from the sea and living things

In cool air the water vapour in clouds **condenses** and water falls down as rain and snow. The water flows downwards through the ground. It goes into rivers and streams and flows back to the sea.

Water soaks into the ground or flows into rivers and lakes on its way to the sea

Short water cycle

In some places water **evaporates** and **condenses** in a short time. In rainforests it is hot during the day so water evaporates very quickly.

Rain falls every day on the forest and down to the ground.

The rain helps plants in the rainforest to grow very well.

At night it is much cooler in the rainforests and clouds form. The **water vapour** condenses and falls as rain. The rain evaporates and so the cycle goes round again.

25

Long water cycle

In very cold places it takes longer for water to **evaporate** and **condense**. Water droplets in clouds **freeze** and fall as snow. Then the snow changes to ice.

Rivers carry ice slowly to the sea where it melts.

Ice slowly melts when the Sun is shining on it.

In cold places ice does not **melt**. Sometimes huge pieces of ice move into warmer water. Here they melt and the water evaporates. The cycle goes round again.

27

Salty to fresh

The water in the sea is salty. The water in mountain streams is not salty. It is fresh water. When seawater **evaporates**, the salt is left behind.

Salt can sometimes be seen on the skin after swimming in the sea.

The water in a mountain spring is clean and pure.

When water goes back to the sea, fresh water mixes with salty water. The water changes from fresh to salty.

Salt test

This simple test will show **evaporation**. Place a saucer of salty water by a window or radiator and leave it there for two or three days. What do you think will happen?

The water will evaporate but the salt will be left behind in the saucer. This is what happens to the water in seas and oceans.

  Find out more about Nature's Patterns at www.heinemannexplore.co.uk

Glossary

condense when a gas changes into liquid

evaporate when liquid changes into a gas

freeze turn into ice

gas like air, not a liquid or solid

humid warm and damp

ice crystal small piece of ice

invisible cannot be seen

liquid something that flows or can be poured

melt changing from a solid to a liquid due to heat

pattern something that happens over and over again

solid firm, not liquid

surface area on the top of something

water vapour gas that has been changed from water

More books to read

Materials: Water, Chris Oxlade (Heinemann Library, 2003)

My World of Science: Water, Angela Royston (Heinemann Library, 2001)

Watching the Weather: Rain, Elisabeth Miles (Heinemann Library, 2004)

Index